Overthinking

A Step-by-Step Guide to Master Your Emotions

with 49 Powerful Motivational

Quotes to Unlock Your Potential

ZACHARY MILLER

Table of Contents

Introduction

Congratulations on purchasing Stop Overthinking and thank you for doing so.
The following chapters will discuss how you can stop overthinking, take control of your thoughts, and reduce your worrying and anxiety. You will be able to reduce negativity in your life and manage your stress more effectively, allowing you to enjoy your life and live in the present moment. You will establish new habits for yourself and achieve new results as a result of it.

In this book, you will learn how to focus. This involves decluttering your mind, practicing minimalism, taking steps to improve your focus, and learning the proper way to prioritize so that you focus on what matters the most to you. You will learn how to stop worrying once and for all so that it no longer controls your life. This means that you can live in the present moment, stop the constant "what-ifs," and become more aware of your thoughts and actions. This book also focuses on relieving anxiety, preventing future anxiety by establishing healthy habits, and becoming more aware of your mental health so that you can improve it. You will learn to eliminate negativity, stop complaining, find positivity in your life, and identify the sources of your negativity so that you can prevent it in the future.

Mindfulness is another important topic. This involves defining mindfulness and what it entails, learning how to practice it, how to incorporate it into your life, and the benefits of practicing mindfulness. You will learn how to become the master of your mind by riding your emotional waves, manipulating your mindset, and controlling your thoughts. This will help you to think and act the way you want and allow you to have full control of your life instead of letting your mind control you.

The next focus is on overthinking and how to prevent it. The book will answer the question of what overthinking is, help you understand if you struggle with overthinking, teach you how to stop yourself from it, and show you what habits you can establish to prevent it.

Another important topic is how to avoid letting others use their power to bring you down. To prevent this, you must understand how to defend yourself verbally, how to take control of your own mind instead of allowing others to do so, choose the right people to surround yourself with, and eliminate those who bring you down. Eliminating stress is also discussed. You will learn how to fight against stress, some strategies for reducing stress, habits to establish to relieve your stress, and how to recognize stressors in your life. Finally, you will learn a few tips and tricks for maximizing your full potential and improving yourself. You will learn some tips on how to improve your health (both physical and mental). You will also read about some other tips for getting in the proper mindset, getting into new habits, and setting proper goals.

There are numerous books available on this particular topic, and I am grateful that you have chosen this one. We have put in a lot of effort to ensure that this book is packed with valuable information that can benefit you, and we hope that you enjoy reading it.

Chapter 1: Learn to Focus

These days, there are so many topics that your mind can be focused on. You constantly get alerts on your phone. There's always more work to do. There are places to be, people to see, and a never-ending list of tasks to accomplish. However, it's important to learn how to focus. This way, you will be able to place your attention on the task at hand and give your all to it. You may often find yourself caught up in what's coming next or dwelling on the past. However, you must be able to train your brain to focus on what needs your attention the most.

It's important to declutter your mind by eliminating unnecessary thoughts to make space for what truly matters. Embracing minimalism in your life can help you prioritize and focus on what you value most. Learning how to concentrate is also crucial. There are various techniques to make this easier, such as prioritizing your tasks and putting them down in writing. This creates a visual representation of your most important goals and helps you stay focused, reducing the overwhelm caused by endless thoughts.

Decluttering Your Mind

Decluttering your mind is crucial for your mental health, productivity, and concentration. A cluttered mind can disrupt your sleep, hinder your ability to focus on work, and prevent you from enjoying your life due to constant worries and endless thoughts. Luckily, there are several effective ways to declutter your mind and regain control of your thoughts.

There are several ways to declutter your mind and improve your mental health, productivity, and ability to concentrate. One of the ways is to declutter your physical space. A cluttered workspace or home can lead to mental overwhelm and distract you from focusing on important tasks. Take time to go through your space and get rid of anything you don't need. Surround yourself with an environment that helps you focus instead of hindering your focus.

Another way to declutter your mind is to avoid multitasking. It may seem like a way to get more done, but splitting your focus among several tasks leads to lower quality work and feeling overwhelmed. Make it a habit to completely finish one task before moving onto another.

Being decisive is also important to declutter your mind. Instead of putting tasks off until later, decide what to do at the moment. If you struggle with making a decision, jot down the potential pros and cons of each choice to guide you in the decision-making process. Eliminate tasks that don't matter and make a schedule for routine tasks to reduce the number of decisions you have to make.

Preparing ahead of time can also help declutter your mind. Plan your outfits for the week, meal-prep, and make a schedule for routine tasks like laundry and vacuuming. Reducing decisions and having a schedule can help stop overthinking and allow you to focus on what's important.

Sunday	Monday	Tuesday	Wednesday	Thursday	Friday	Saturday
Pick clothes	Bathroom	Dishes	Vacuum	Laundry	Trash	Meal-prep

Minimalism

Minimalism, typically regarded as an intense trend, is actually quite helpful for those who wish to focus more clearly. Although there are some that take this to the extreme and live out of a suitcase and choose to not have a home or car, minimalism is a practice of being more mindful of what you choose to keep in your life. It can be applied across your life to help you to only have what matters to you in your life. You may find yourself practicing minimalism in one area of your life, only to have that affect other areas of your life.

Minimalism isn't simply getting rid of things or decluttering your belongings. It is seeing what truly matters to you and sticking with that. Marie Kondo's method is to only keep items that "spark joy." This means that you only keep the items in your life that truly make you happy. It can really help you to go through each item that you own and decide what matters to you. You may have some things that you keep out of guilt or for "someday in the future." However, these items will only disappoint and frustrate you each time you see them. It is important to eliminate any items that bring you negativity or remind you of failure. Surround yourself with items that bring you joy and make you a better person. Your surroundings should be a reflection of you and what you love. You may choose to go through the items in your house, at work, in your car, and any other places that you may have. Do not bring any other items into your life that bring you down in any way; only own what you truly need to make you happy. This can help you to have a much clearer mind.

Additionally, you may practice digital minimalism. You may feel overwhelmed with the amount of information that you have coming in. There will constantly be e-mails, texts, and other notifications. Social media can also be quite overwhelming. Delete any apps that you don't use or that you don't find happiness from. Get rid of that educational app that you "should" be using but never do. Get rid of those storage-sucking apps that you don't like. Clean up your phone. Turn off notifications that you don't need. You may go through your e-mails and delete all the ones you don't need. Unsubscribe from e-mails. Create a labeling system. For social media, unfollow those who don't have a positive effect on your life. You may even choose to stop using social media or go on a social media detox. Limit yourself to a certain amount of time for social media. There is so much information that comes from social media, and much of it is unnecessary. Make sure that you are spending your time the way you want to be spending it.

Learning to Focus

Begin by reflecting on your focus and assessing how satisfied you are with your ability to concentrate. Do you feel that your focus could use some improvement? Identify what your specific goal is, and pinpoint the factors that tend to hinder your ability to focus. Do you struggle with getting easily distracted, taking breaks that last too long, or completing tasks efficiently?

Challenge yourself to a task and a time limit, and pay close attention to how often you become distracted and how easily you can regain your focus. Jot down any potential distractions, as it can be difficult to identify them in the moment. Once you've identified them, make a plan to eliminate them. Turn off notifications, find a quiet space, or do whatever it takes to create an environment conducive to focused work. Experiment with different schedules for breaks to determine what works best for you. Perhaps you prefer shorter breaks more frequently, or a longer break after a longer period of work. Regular breaks can help to reduce stress and increase productivity.

Reflect on what triggers your loss of focus and overthinking. What are the root causes of these issues? Developing an awareness of these triggers can help you to avoid them or address them when they occur.

There are several techniques you can use to improve your focus. Meditation is one effective method for training your mind to be calm and present in the moment. It may take time to get comfortable with it, but it can have numerous benefits for your mental and emotional well-being, including improving your ability to concentrate. Engaging in physical activity can also help you to refocus your mind and reduce tension. Regular exercise can have a positive impact on your physical health, which can in turn improve your mental health and concentration.

Remember to take care of yourself by getting enough sleep, eating well, and staying hydrated. When you feel good physically and mentally, it will be easier to maintain your focus and be productive. Finally, taking time for yourself and doing activities that bring you joy can help to reduce stress and increase motivation, leading to better focus and overall well-being.

Prioritizing

Sometimes, it's not a lack of focus that's the issue, but rather a lack of focus on the right things. It's easy to get sidetracked by tasks that are unimportant or not urgent, and you might think you're being productive when in reality you're just procrastinating. That's why prioritization is crucial; you need to be able to identify where your focus should be placed. Otherwise, it's like running on a treadmill - you're expending energy, but you're not really getting anywhere. To make sure you're making progress, you must learn to prioritize your tasks and focus on the important ones first.

One helpful way to prioritize is by creating a to-do list every day, preferably the night before. This way, you can plan ahead and have a clear idea of what you need to accomplish. Even if you're not feeling particularly motivated at the moment, it's important to identify one to three major tasks for the day - these are your top priorities. Even if these are the only things you accomplish, you'll be satisfied with your progress because you've focused on what's truly important. So make sure to prioritize your tasks and focus on the ones that will help you achieve your goals.

You should also write down any additional goals that you have for the day. Write every possible thing that is on your mind. Make a list of all of the potential tasks, even if they aren't necessary for the day. By doing a "brain dump," you are freeing yourself of clutter in your mind. This will really help you to focus on the present instead of the past or future. Additionally, you will feel better knowing that you won't forget anything that you would like to do. It will all be written down, so you can feel more at peace.

Brain Dump
Need to do progress towards completing a project, go grocery shopping, go to the bank, clean kitchen, take the dog to the groomer, do laundry and wash sheets, go to the gym, talk to sister about dinner, schedule dentist appointment, etc.

You may also consider journaling to help you figure out what matters. Each day, you may reflect on your day. Determine what your strengths and weaknesses for that day were. How was your focus? Did you accomplish everything? This will also help you to determine how you can improve for the next day. Although it will take time to become better at focusing, you may practice and improve your skills every day. Eventually, you will naturally prioritize your tasks and focus. Until then, you must make a conscious effort to do so.

Prioritizing your tasks will allow you to accomplish what is urgent and important first. Tasks with deadlines or of greater importance will be completed first. By doing this, you are allowing yourself to not feel guilty, as you will complete what you must before moving onto less urgent and less important activities. You can even reward yourself with some fun after completing your daily tasks. When you procrastinate, you are clouding your focus and delaying the completion of important tasks. You are hindering your performance and missing out on opportunities. When you learn how to focus, you will feel much better and will reduce your overthinking tendencies.

It's very important to learn how to focus. You are likely overwhelmed with all of the information that you receive, all of the tasks that you must complete, and all of the thoughts in your head. Each day brings new surprises and new information with it. It's important to be able to have a filter on it to allow yourself to focus on what you must. Otherwise, you will constantly feel anxious, stress, and overwhelmed by all of the thoughts in your head. This will lead to overthinking, as you will think about the potential tasks to complete and won't have a plan for it. As a result, you won't be able to enjoy the present moment because you are so focused on your past failures and worried about making future mistakes. However, learning to focus can really help you.

Decluttering your mind will help you to remove all of your unnecessary thoughts. You will learn how to focus on what matters so that you may direct your energy towards that. Similarly, practicing minimalism will help you to understand what you value in life. You will realize what you should put your focus on, and what you find important. You can learn to focus by means of a few methods. Physical and mental health will play a huge role in your ability to focus. Finally, prioritizing will help you to learn what you should focus your attention on. You will feel more at ease when you can focus on what you need to.

Chapter 2: Stop Worrying

We all worry from time to time. You worry about yourself and others on a daily basis. This is normal, to an extent. You may worry about the potential of failure, about your safety, or other possible factors. It is instinctual, as animals must worry about their hunger until they feed themselves. However, there is a certain point where worrying is unhealthy. If you find yourself constantly worrying to the extent where it takes over your life, you need to take action. You must be able to enjoy your life. While you will certainly worry occasionally, it should not prevent you from completing your daily tasks. When worrying becomes severe, it needs attention.

You must learn to stop worrying. There is always the chance of a negative event occurring, but you must be able to find positivity and hope instead of dwelling on the potential for something going wrong. You must be able to live in the moment and focus on enjoying yourself instead of worrying about what you did incorrectly in the past and what could go wrong in the future. You must be able to enjoy your life, not spend every minute of it worrying. It's important to be able to stop the "what-ifs" and develop the ability to focus on the best possible outcome. There is a good balance between being realistic and being positive, and you must be able to find that balance. You should also become more aware of yourself and your emotions.

Stop Worrying

It sounds simple enough: just stop worrying. Although this seems easier said than done, it is possible to train your brain to worry less and be able to enjoy yourself more. Worrying can be lessened, and you may greatly minimize it and even prevent it from occurring. However, this will take a lot of practice and patience with your progress. If you tend to worry naturally, this will be an ingrained habit that will take time to replace with better habits. You must be able to change your mind so that you may reduce the amount of worrying that you do.

There are a few ways that you can reduce the amount of time that you spend worrying. One way is to simply set aside time to worry. Instead of suppressing your worries and ignoring them until they reach the point where they overwhelm you, set aside time each day to simply let your emotions happen. Instead of fighting against them, allow yourself to feel everything. You may even imagine yourself overreacting; this will allow you to see how beneficial (or not) it can be to allow your emotions to take over. Spending some time each day just letting it out will help you. You may choose to keep a journal or simply write everything down. Perhaps you type it out all of your thoughts and erase it right afterward so that you can see a clearing of your thoughts right in front of you. You may choose to confide in someone you trust, allowing yourself to rant for a few minutes to get it all out. Regardless, it is healthy to let your emotions out instead of suppressing them.

Determine the root of your worries. Perhaps you have too much free time and simply need something else to occupy your mind. You may choose to take up a hobby to keep yourself busy. There may be a particular event that triggers your worries. You may feel worried while scrolling through social media, as you compare yourself to others and worry that you aren't good enough. Perhaps your worries are the result of a past trauma that you still haven't moved on from. No matter the cause, it is important to take some time to reflect on why it is that you worry and work on a solution for that.

Another aspect to consider is whether your worries are solvable or not. If the worry has a solution, come up with a way to solve it and get it done. Instead of dwelling on it, solve it so that you may have more peace of mind. For worries that are unsolvable, you must be willing to accept that fact. Instead of trying to predict negative events or worrying about possibilities with a low likelihood, accept the uncertainty. Will worrying solve it or change it? The answer is most likely "no." Worrying won't prevent unpleasant surprises. You must be willing to accept the fact that life constantly changes. Finding the good in these changes can really help you to be happier and stress less.

Live in the Moment

Learning to live in the moment can really help you to stop worrying. Often, worrying is a result of the past or future. We don't typically worry as much about what we are doing in the present. You must be willing to accept the past and live without regrets. Every mistake is a learning opportunity, and every issue will only make you stronger. The future is unpredictable; the best you can do is to work your hardest towards making it a future you want.

However, that's pretty difficult when you spend your time worrying!

You must learn to enjoy the present, or else you will never enjoy your life. Otherwise, you will always wish that you are in the past or be hoping to have a better life in the future. Tomorrow never comes, though. It will always be today. As a result, you must learn the importance of living today. Focus on the present. Be aware of all of the positive aspects of the present. To do this, you may have to shut off your electronic devices and really take in your surroundings. Take a moment to realize how great the present is and be more mindful. Accept your thoughts of the present, while allowing yourself to shut off thoughts about the past or future. Become aware of your senses. What are you seeing, hearing, smelling, feeling, and tasting? Instead of constantly multitasking, take a moment to appreciate what you are doing.

You may appreciate the finer details in life. Be thankful for small moments and what you may have previously neglected. There is much more to life than the obvious. The smallest details can make the biggest difference in your happiness. Appreciate everything, even the smallest aspects of life.

You may live in the moment by being happier and bringing joy to others. Remember to laugh and smile. These can really boost your happiness and help you to enjoy life more. Bring happiness to others, as well. Volunteering and performing small acts of kindness can go a long way. You will feel happy knowing that you made a difference and have a purpose. Be thankful for everything that you have and be sure to help others that may need help as well. Occasionally take a moment to realize everything that you are thankful for. Find positivity every day.

Take small moments to yourself. Perhaps you may choose to meditate. You may also simply breathe and focus on your breath. Focus on how your body feels and take some time to relax. You may feel that you can't enjoy the present because you are too overwhelmed. Check with yourself regularly and remind yourself to live in the present. You will have to make a conscious effort to do this at first, as it is natural to visualize the future or dwell on the past. When you can live in the present, you will learn to enjoy life no matter how it is.

Stop the "What-Ifs"

There are so many possible "what-ifs" that you can have. If you tend to worry constantly, you are bound to believe that the worst will happen. However, this thinking does not get you anywhere. If you constantly assume the worst and expect the worst, you will lack the motivation to continue on. You will feel like there is no point, as you will expect the worst to occur. It is therefore important for you to stop this cycle and to view life in a positive way. Although it is important to be realistic, you can't always expect the worst.

There is a proper balance between being realistic and being positive. You can't always get your hopes up for everything; it won't help you to have wildly unrealistic expectations, as you will feel disappointed constantly. However, you also can't approach life as something that's pointless and think that something will always go wrong. Although you may feel that this is more realistic, you must be willing to accept that life will be full of both challenges and successes. If you only focus on one, you are missing out. Mistakes and hardships will teach you more about yourself, others, and life in general. If life didn't have problems, the good times wouldn't be as great. You must be willing to take the bad with the good, and it's important to accept that both of these will occur. Doing so will allow you to live a life that is less worry-filled and full of more happiness.

Everyone experiences "what-if" thoughts from time to time. This is normal and can help with the decision-making process. However, they can harm your daily life when they start to interfere with your routine. If you struggle to go about your everyday routine because you are too focused on the potential for negativity, you need to make changes to yourself regarding your worrying. When you can't control your thoughts, it's problematic.

To control these thoughts, you can try a few methods. One way is to write down these thoughts when they occur. By doing so, you are becoming more informed of how you think, and you may realize that these thoughts lack logic behind them. It will help you to realize what you are thinking, and you may understand why you think that way as a result. You should also take action on these thoughts. If there is a way to solve the problem that you are worried about, do it. If there isn't, find a way to let go of that thought. Talk to someone, write it down, or think it through. You may also take a moment to understand what the thought is, how it makes you feel, and what your reaction to it is. This will help you to have a better emotional response to it and behave properly to solve the issue. You must also become more comfortable with change and uncertainty. Recognize that some things will simply remain unknown until they occur and worrying will not alter the outcome.

Become More Aware of Yourself

Self-awareness can really help you. It can make it much easier for you to understand your emotions and feel more in control of your mind. You will realize why you act and think the way that you do. You can understand what your strengths and weaknesses are. It will also help you realize what motivates you. You will become more aware of your purpose and goals in life. It can even help you to understand others better and improve your communication skills. By increasing your self-awareness, you will have a healthier mind and feel much better about yourself and your emotions.

To become more self-aware, you will have to make a conscious effort to do so at first. Take some time each day to really reflect on how you are feeling. Understand your current emotions, the causes of them, and the effect they have on you. You may also reflect on your day as a whole. Did you accomplish what you set out to do? If not, what held you back from doing so? Use this time to constructively criticize yourself. Do not simply criticize yourself, compare yourself to others, or think about how you failed. Instead, realize what worked for you and what did not. Doing so will benefit you, as you can learn from that and apply it to the next day. You will not be perfect at first, but if you can make improvements each day, you will be much better off. Only compare yourself to who you were yesterday. You should always be learning, improving, and changing for the better. This is a natural way to progress in life, and it's important to do so to be the best person that you possibly can be. Remember to think about both what can be improved and what you did well, as it is important to remind yourself of your successes and remember that you are capable of success.

You may ask others to help you in several ways. One way is to talk out your emotions with another that you trust. This can help you to verbally express your thoughts. You may also ask others for feedback, as they will be able to give you an opinion outside of yourself. However, this must be healthy. You should trust the other person's word and ensure that you take everything they say as a way to improve, not as an attack on the person that you are. It's also important that you are able to write down your values and goals. This will make you more aware of what you're working towards. If you don't have goals to work towards, you will lack both direction and a sense of purpose in life. Understand what is important to you and what gives you a sense of importance. If you don't have goals, you won't be able to reflect on your progress towards achieving your goals. As a result, you won't be able to be aware of how you are doing.

Worrying can really hold you back from your full potential. Instead of living your life enjoying it, you will be spending your time worrying. For this reason, it's crucial that you work on minimizing the amount of worrying that you do. In addition to feeling happier, you will be less stressed and anxious. You will feel a weight lifted off of your shoulders as well. It will be easier for you to focus on what matters instead of dwelling on what doesn't matter. You will find greater importance in life and be able to concentrate on what matters to you. At work, you will feel more capable of accomplishing your daily tasks. At home, you will feel a better connection with those around you. While you are out and about, you will be able to go about your day without feeling overwhelmed with worries.

It's important to stop your habit of worrying, and there are a few ways that you can work on it. You must, however, keep in mind that it will take work to stop yourself from worrying. It's also important to discover how to live in the moment so that you can enjoy life and feel greater happiness. Stopping the "what-ifs" that you think can really help you. Most of these are unnecessary, and you will feel better for not thinking these thoughts. Finally, you must become more aware of yourself to worry less.

Chapter 3: Relieving Anxiety

We all get anxious from time to time. You get anxious before speaking in front of others, before an important meeting, for an interview, and other such events. However, those with anxiety feel anxious so much to the point where it interferes with their daily lives. Anxiety can prevent you from being able to go about your daily routine. It can stop you from wanting to get out of the house or even out of bed. You will lose motivation, feel unworthy, and simply won't be happy. However, there are a few ways that you can help yourself and make your anxiety much more manageable.

There are some ways to relieve your anxiety. This will make it much easier to cope with, and you will feel much better as a result. It will allow you to take control of yourself again. It's also important to recognize anxiety. Realizing what triggers, you and the potential causes of your anxiety can help you in resolving any issues that you may have. You may not even realize what causes your anxiety, or that you struggle with it in the first place. It's important to be able to distinguish between what's normal and what isn't. You may also work to improve your overall mental health, which can improve your anxiety levels and help you to feel happier and more emotionally stable. Finally, there are several habits that you can incorporate into your life to help you to work on preventing anxiety in the future.

Anxiety Relief

Anxiety can be difficult. When it begins to interfere with your life, it can create many challenges and prevent you from living your life to its full potential. Although it is important to seek the help of a medical professional when needed, there are several ways that you can work on relieving your anxiety yourself. You may try these ways before seeking the help of a professional. Little changes can make a big difference in your anxiety, and it's possible to fully help yourself to feel better. There are a few things that you can try to relieve your anxiety.

One way to help your anxiety is by taking care of your physical health. Your physical health has both a direct and indirect relationship with your mental health. If your body is functioning better overall, your brain will be functioning better too. You will be able to better regulate your hormones when you take care of yourself, so your emotions and thoughts will be healthier. Taking care of your physical health will indirectly help your anxiety as well. There will be much less to feel anxious about. When you take care of yourself, you will feel more confident in yourself and feel more capable of achieving your goals. You won't feel as anxious about your health, as you can feel confident knowing that you take care of yourself. Additionally, you won't care as much how other people think of you. You will feel better about yourself and won't feel as insecure as you once did.

Taking time to relax can also help you to relieve your anxiety. Find what helps you to feel calmer and incorporate that into your daily routine. For some, this can be a walk around the park. It may be unwinding in the bath while reading a book. You may have a hobby that helps you to relax. No matter what it is, ensure that you incorporate some sort of relaxation into your day. Every day should have some time for you to be quiet, focus, and relax. Meditation can provide individuals with great benefits, as it eases the mind and provides those who do so with a sense of calmness. This is very easy and free to do, and there are many guided meditations available to explore both online and in-person. If you aren't one to meditate, even taking some time to practice deep breathing can help you to calm down and feel more relaxed. This will have you be more mindful of your body and turn your focus away from the outside world while instead concentrating on yourself. Taking slow and deep breaths will help you with your anxiety. Certain smells can also relieve anxiety. Essential oils such as lavender, grapefruit, and sage can be added to a bath, around your home, or into a diffuser to increase your relaxation and help with your anxiety even more. Relieving your anxiety doesn't have to be complicated or expensive. Simply taking care of yourself and giving yourself time to relax can have a huge impact on your anxiety and really benefit you.

Healthy Habits for Preventing Anxiety

You can also incorporate some good habits into your life to help with your anxiety. These habits are all simple and will help you to feel better and live a healthier life. In addition to taking time to yourself every day and relaxing, you can incorporate a few habits into your life that consist of taking care of your physical health. These will also have a positive impact on your anxiety.

One habit to incorporate into your daily routine is exercising. Whether you like to go to the gym, go for a run, bike, swim, or play a sport, exercising is great. It can help you to get your body moving. You will feel much better, and it is a good way to take care of your body. It can also help you to have a better sense of well-being and feel better. It is a great way to distract yourself from negative thoughts and give you something to look forward to every day, especially if you choose an activity that you like.

Another important habit is eating well every day. Watching your diet can have a huge impact on your health. When you fuel your body with the right foods, your body will reward you by feeling much better. You will feel energized and more motivated to accomplish whatever you set your mind to. Your body runs off of the foods that you put in it, so make sure that you are putting the right foods in your body to experience the best performance possible.

Additionally, you should be drinking the right drinks. Getting enough water every day is important so that you stay hydrated and are feeling the best that you can. You may consider adding in a cup of chamomile tea to your daily routine, as it is known for its calming effect on the body. Sugary drinks should be minimized, as they will only give you a short boost of energy followed by a "crash," where you will feel drained and unmotivated. Similarly, caffeine should be avoided, as it has a negative effect on those with anxiety. If you struggle with anxiety, it is important to focus on calming your body, whereas caffeine will have the opposite effect on you. Likewise, it is also best to avoid alcohol, as it provides users with similar effects.

You should also sleep properly each night. This means that you should get the proper amount of sleep. It's also helpful to stick to a sleep schedule, as it will help your body to become used to going to bed and waking up at the same time. Those with anxiety often struggle with falling asleep. To help this, it's wise to avoid electronics an hour before bed. You may come up with a nightly routine, such as reading, taking a shower, and generally unwinding for the hour before bedtime. This will get you in the right mindset for sleeping and tell your body that it's time to rest. Make sure that your room is also sleep-friendly. It should be quiet, cool, and comfortable. Leave your phone off or in another room, and make sure that your room is dark. This will help you to sleep better.

Recognizing Anxiety

Learning to recognize anxiety is important. It can help you realize if you need to work on yourself and make changes to yourself. You may not realize that your anxiety is having such a profound impact on your life, and it may motivate you to seek the help of yourself or others. You may also learn to recognize your anxiety so that you can determine when you are experiencing a wave of anxiety and what the cause of that wave is. Overall, it can prove highly beneficial for you to learn how to recognize if and when you are experiencing anxiety.

Although it is normal to feel anxious sometimes, there is a difference between feeling anxious once in a while and struggling with anxiety. While you may experience signs of anxiety before an important event, during a circumstance that makes you nervous, or after taking a risk, anxiety is more than that. It involves a constant cycle of worry and fear. It may have you feeling extreme terror as a result of everyday situations. Everyone is different, and the waves of anxiety tend to be quite random and uncontrollable. You may determine what triggers your anxiety and work to avoid those situations, people, and places so that you can feel less anxious.

Those experiencing anxiety can feel many symptoms and signs regarding their anxiety. This can include a feeling of nervousness or tension, restlessness, increased heart rate, sweating, hyperventilating, and trembling. They may also feel fatigue, inability to concentrate or sleep, digestive issues, or a general sense of uneasiness. Of course, there are some rational reasons to experience anxiety. For instance, you may feel anxious before an interview. You want to impress the interviewer, get the job, and make more money. This is normal, and many others feel the same way. However, it's when you experience these symptoms seemingly "out of nowhere." If there is no logical cause, then you may struggle with anxiety.

It's important to understand what causes your anxiety, as it will be different for everyone. Anxiety can be caused by a number of issues, including past trauma, stress, personality, mental health issues, genetics, drugs, or alcohol. You may even have a reason that is specific to you. For instance, those with social anxiety find it difficult to go about their social life without experiencing great anxiety while doing so. They may not feel comfortable talking to new people or being in situations where they are forced to interact with others. Although it's normal to be a bit nervous when talking to someone for the first time, it becomes problematic when you avoid all socialization and find it difficult to leave your house out of the fear that you will have to socialize. You must determine what the root of your anxiety is so that you may either combat that fear or avoid situations that trigger your anxiety.

Improving Your Mental Health

Improving your mental health as a whole can positively affect your anxiety. You will be able to think more clearly, have better control over your emotions, and feel less stressed. Your mental health is just as important (if not more important) than your physical health. If you don't have the proper mentality, you won't feel motivated to take care of yourself. For this reason, you must take steps to improve your mental health and keep it in the best shape possible.

One way to improve your mental health is by making a conscious effort to do so. Check with yourself and tell yourself something positive. If you can perceive your life and the events that occur positively, you can feel better about those. Find the good in every situation and remind yourself what you are grateful for. Tell yourself something good that happened every day. Instead of only focusing on failures, mistakes, and negative aspects of every day, think and feel the happiness around you. It will take time to develop this skill, but if you make a conscious effort to focus on the positives around you, you will be able to think this way subconsciously. Don't neglect the details; sometimes, the smallest details are what make the biggest differences.

Become more mindful of the present. You may become bored with the same routine every day or fail to see the joys of a task that is seemingly unimportant. However, you must pay attention to the sights, smells, tastes, feelings, and sounds that surround you. This will keep you focused on the present and will reduce the urge to worry. It's a great way to snap back to reality instead of getting caught up in your thoughts. For instance, you may simply take a shower to clean yourself every day. However, when's the last time you really enjoyed taking a shower? Take a moment to breathe in while the water refreshes your body. You may take a few extra seconds to really wash your hair and enjoy the relaxing feeling of it. Think about how great it feels to be clean and refreshed. Appreciating the little things in life can go a long way.

If you feel yourself becoming stressed or overwhelmed, do something about it. Don't ignore the messages that your body is sending you. It is okay to take a break if you are feeling overwhelmed. Although you may feel that you are taking yourself away from the task and accomplishing less, you are actually doing yourself a favor. If you keep pushing past the point where your body is okay, you will only hurt yourself and feel unmotivated and unable to concentrate. Take a walk, talk to someone, write down your feelings, or just breathe.

Anxiety can be challenging to face, and it can have a great effect on your life. Although everyone experiences some form of anxiety from time to time, it is important to know when anxiety is more than just simply feeling nervous about an important event or being apprehensive about trying something new. Anxiety, when severe, can prevent you from functioning properly and hinder your ability to be productive. It can really bring you down and stop you from living your life to the fullest. As a result, it is crucial to take care of yourself when you experience or struggle with any form of anxiety that you may have.

It's important to try to relieve your anxiety the best that you can. This can be quite simple, and you can try a few quick ways to relieve your anxiety yourself. You can also try incorporating healthy habits into your daily routine to help you with your anxiety. It's critical that you are able to recognize anxiety. You should recognize if you struggle with anxiety and to what extent that you do. It's also important to determine when you are experiencing a wave of anxiety so that you may be able to understand what your mind and body are trying to tell you. Knowing how to recognize anxiety can also help you to determine the cause of your anxiety and what may trigger it. You must also take care of your mental health as a whole. Doing so will help you to feel better and help with your anxiety.

Chapter 4: Erasing Negativity

Negativity is all around us. There are constantly others who share their negativity. Social media has become a center for negativity. It can be tempting to join those who are negative and add to their thoughts. You may also feel overwhelmed by your own negative thoughts. They may take over your mind and leave you unable to find the positives. You may feel like failure is inevitable. You may think that you aren't good enough. You may even think that there is nothing good in life. However, you must be able to eliminate negativity, as it will only leave you unmotivated and unproductive. Others don't enjoy the presence of someone who is constantly negative, too. By being more positive, you can improve your relationship with others, yourself, and your work. It can help you to make better progress towards achieving your goals and enjoying your life much more.

It is crucial to eliminate negativity, and there are a few ways that you can do so. It will take patience and effort, yet it will certainly pay off. You must also be able to stop complaining, as complaining will only hurt yourself and further your negative thoughts. It will also be unpleasant for those around you. Although it may take effort, you must also be able to find positivity in your life and in everyday circumstances. You must also realize what the causes of negativity are so that you can avoid getting caught up in negativity and become a more positive person.

Eliminate Negativity

It is important to be able to erase negativity from your life. You may not even realize that you have unnecessary negativity in your life. It's possible that you're so used to it and don't even realize the effect that it has on you. However, you must take a moment to determine what (if anything) is causing negativity in your life. Is there anything, anyone, or anywhere that always results in you feeling sad, frustrated, angry, or disappointed? Perhaps there's a certain place you visit that always gets you down. There may be a person in your life that leaves you feeling unhappy every time you talk to them or spend time with them. There may even be a part of your daily routine that you simply don't enjoy. Regardless, you should pinpoint what exactly causes negative thoughts and leaves you feeling down. The next step is to eliminate those from your life.

One source of negativity to eliminate is any person that causes you negativity. Although you can't make somebody disappear, it's possible to slowly remove them from your life. It's okay to say no to people. You aren't obligated to spend time with anybody. You can remain civil with people without having to be friends with them. This is important to remember for people that you must see, such as co-workers or certain family members. The people that you surround yourself with have a huge impact on your life, your success, and your motivation. Choose wisely. You should be friends with those who inspire you, motivate you, and make you happy. If there is someone in your life that is a poor influence, causes you to think negative thoughts, or is not motivating, you don't have to be around them.

It's also important to eliminate places that cause you negativity. First, you may start with the places you visit the most. Your home should be comforting. It should be a safe space where you can relax, sleep, and live. If you feel unhappy in your home, you may want to consider switching it around a bit. Brighten up your space with some color, your favorite things, and light. Your work environment should allow you to feel productive and motivated. Get rid of anything that disallows these. The places that you visit should also make you happy. If you don't like going somewhere, then don't go! It's worth a little extra time and money to pick places that make you happy.

You should also eliminate negativity from your daily routine. If there is something that you don't enjoy doing but feel pressured to do, try to find a way around it, a way to eliminate it, or a way to make it better. For instance, you may scroll through social media for hours each day and feel guilty about it. It may leave you feeling negative because everyone either bragging or complaining. You may feel that you "need" to do it due to an addiction to it or out of fear that you'll miss out on something. However, those that matter will call you, message you, or see you in person. There are other ways to get news. You may set a timer for how long each day you'll allow yourself to use social media, or you may cut it off altogether. You may also switch the social media that you use.

Stop Complaining

Just stop complaining! It sounds easy enough, doesn't it? Complaining can become ingrained in your brain. It may even be your automatic reaction to events or your way of coping. It's important to realize that complaining will not help the situation, though. In fact, it can make it harder to deal with, as you will be caught up in the negative aspects of each situation. There are a few ways to train yourself to stop complaining, yet you must realize that it will take time, patience, and effort. This is especially true if complaining has become a habit.

One way to stop complaining is to become more comfortable with change. One great mindset to adopt is that "everything happens for a reason." Even if you aren't religious or spiritual, you can acknowledge the fact that you are only here because of everything that happened before you. People come into your life and teach you lessons only for them to be gone the next day. An opportunity will arise, and it may not work out. However, it didn't work out because another, better opportunity was waiting for you. You can't let change get you down. You must be able and willing to accept the fact that life doesn't follow a plan. Thinking this way can really help you, and you may train yourself to respond better to change. To do so, you can force yourself to try new things. Go explore a new place, eat new foods, and spend time with someone that you normally don't. You may try a new hobby. By allowing yourself to become comfortable with change (and learn to like it), you will respond much better when life doesn't go according to plan. This will help you realize that there is so much out there waiting for you, and you don't know if you'll like it until you try it.

You may also develop an awareness of your complaining. Perhaps you can tell others to call you out for it when you do it. You may not realize how much you complain. When you do find yourself complaining, ask yourself some questions. Why am I complaining? What benefit does complaining give me and others? Is there a better way to respond to this situation? By reflecting on your complaining, you can snap yourself back to reality and really consider if complaining is a good response or not.

Learn to express your dissatisfaction in another way. Although complaining is a bad habit, it doesn't mean that you should allow yourself to be taken advantage of. If you are unhappy with something, it can be beneficial to tell someone about it so they can improve the situation. It may be as simple as being polite. For instance, you may have to return a broken item at a store. Instead of complaining to the customer service representative about how awful of an experience you had, how you hate the store, and how much of an inconvenience it was to you, don't. It isn't their fault that it was broken. Mistakes happen. You may simply explain that it is broken and either ask for a replacement or to return the item. This will allow you to have a better mentality, as you will accept that a mistake has been made and the issue is being resolved. It will make others respect you more, and you are more likely to get what you want as a result. On the other hand, complaining leads to unhappiness and can confuse others on what it is that you want from them.

Find Positivity

A great way to stop complaining is by replacing it with positivity. Every time you catch yourself complaining, replace it with a positive thought. For instance, you may have to wait in a long line at the bank. Instead of complaining about how it's a waste of time, you could be doing other things on your to-do list, and how it's irritating, you can remember the positives of the situation. Perhaps it is a relief to you. Instead of constantly moving about, you now have some time to yourself to think and reflect. You can use this time to check your e-mails, which you previously didn't have time for. Instead of making a big deal out of every small inconvenience and issue that you face, find the positive aspects of it. Remember that there is always something to be grateful for and that happiness can be found everywhere around you.

Train yourself to be more positive. You can start off by reassuring yourself of your positive aspects. Point out to yourself what your favorite things are about yourself and remember that. This will leave you feeling more confident and prouder of yourself. Perhaps you enjoy a certain physical feature of yourself. You may remind yourself of your talents, your achievements, or a great quality about yourself. When you have positivity in yourself, you will feel confident and others will notice a difference. You will feel more capable of anything that you set your mind to.

You may spread this positivity to others. Complimenting others can make a huge difference. It can help others to be happier, you to feel good about yourself, and work to spread positivity. Compliments don't just have to be about appearance; you can compliment your best friend on how great of a listener they are. You may give a compliment to your co-worker on how well-organized they are. This will help you to see the good in others, and they will be grateful for it.

Once you have mastered this, positivity will come more naturally to you. You can really spread your positivity to others. You may motivate others when they need it. You can perform random acts of kindness and even volunteer for causes that you believe in. Becoming a positive role can really help you to feel good, give you a sense of purpose, and inspire others to be more positive.

You may also cultivate positivity by surrounding yourself with it. This way, you will absorb positivity from your surroundings. Make your home, work, and other places of your own positive. You may fill those spaces with inspirational quotes, fun decorations, and your favorite things. Pictures of loved ones can remind you of your purpose and make you smile. You may incorporate the things that make you happiest into your daily routine. Put your favorite smells around your house or in your car. Allow yourself to have your favorite snack every day at 3:00 pm. Listen to your favorite music. Allow yourself to dance, talk to loved ones, and live your life to its fullest potential. The sights, sounds, smells, tastes, and feelings that surround you can make a huge difference in your happiness. Even just taking ten minutes to make yourself smile every day can change your life for the better. Taking a moment to breathe and relax can prevent you from overreacting to a situation. Refocusing your brain and becoming more mindful can help you to eliminate negativity and replace it with positivity.

Causes of Negativity

There are many causes of negativity, and they will vary from person to person. It's important to identify where your negativity stems from. Is it the people you surround yourself with? Is it any place that you visit? Is it actions that you take every day? It's crucial to identify what causes your negativity so that you can eliminate and prevent further negativity from occurring.

Your negativity may be caused by stress or anxiety. As a way to cope with how you're feeling, you may express it with negativity. When this occurs, you must be able to take a step back and relax. Focus on yourself. Although it may seem unproductive to do so, you will feel much more motivated and will accomplish much more if you pay attention to your body's messages and are able to help yourself.

You may be negative because you lack motivation or are bored with your routine. The way to resolve this is by setting goals for yourself. Give yourself something to look forward to and work towards. This will inspire you and help you to improve yourself. Remember to challenge yourself to always be better than you were yesterday. Your negativity can come from the lack of change in your life. You may not feel that you have accomplished anything recently, and life as a whole may not seem exciting to you. Make plans to try something new. Perhaps you can take up a new hobby or learn a new skill. Make plans to impress yourself. Learn new things and make new accomplishments. Work on setting and achieving goals.

Erasing negativity is crucial for your success and happiness. If you live a life full of negativity, you will only remain stagnant and will be unable to make any progress. You will feel unmotivated, as you will only see the bad side of everything. You won't feel driven, as there won't be anything that you feel passionate about. When you are negative, each day seems to drag on, and there is nothing enjoyable about life. You may not feel the need to take care of yourself, as you feel that it is pointless to do so. As a result, you will be stuck in a cycle of negativity where you feel unimportant and unmotivated. You may also negatively affect those around you, bringing them down and creating a poor impression for yourself. Others may lose respect for you and wish to not be around you.

However, it's possible to eliminate negativity from your life. Although it may take practice, you can eliminate negativity. You may also stop complaining. Although you may have developed a habit of complaining, you can get out of that and start finding positive topics to talk about. You may find positivity in the world around you. This will help you to think and act positively, and you will have much more joy. Finding the cause of your negativity can help you to prevent and avoid triggers of your negativity and leave you happier.

Chapter 5: Practicing Mindfulness

Learning how to practice mindfulness is very important. It can help you to be more aware of yourself and your surroundings. It can really help you to understand your emotions. You can figure out what you are feeling, why you are feeling that way, and how you should respond to those feelings. If you are feeling down, practicing mindfulness can bring you back and help you to find positivity when you need it the most. Being mindful can teach you to pay attention to the smaller details and really live in the moment. It will allow you to live life to the fullest and appreciate everything that life has to offer.

Understanding mindfulness can benefit you by showing you how you may benefit by practicing mindfulness and allowing yourself to become more mindful. Learning to practice mindfulness will teach you how to become a master of your own mind and develop a sense of awareness of both yourself and the world outside of yourself. You may incorporate mindfulness into your life by a few simple and quick habits. It's easy to make your daily routine more mindful and to check in with yourself occasionally and be more mindful of your thoughts, actions, and emotions. To stay motivated on your mindfulness journey, you must recognize and remind yourself of the benefits of mindfulness. You may not have even heard of mindfulness, but it is a great tool to incorporate into your life to make the most of your everyday life.

What is Mindfulness?

To practice mindfulness, you must know what it is and how you can practice it. It is more than simply thinking or having a mind. Mindfulness is the tool that you can use to be fully aware of yourself and your surroundings. It means that you are present in the moment instead of being distracted by the outside world, the past, or the future. Instead of worrying, you will be fully focused on the present. When you are mindful, you will be able to concentrate on what is currently happening. You may realize what it is that you are doing and how that makes you feel.

It is so tempting to get caught up in a number of distractions. Our devices constantly have new notifications on them. There is always a new person to talk to, a new task to complete, or a new place to visit. We get caught up in the shows we watch, the games we play, and everything happening around us. However, it's important to not lose touch with reality. Sometimes, it's crucial to bring your focus back to yourself and really concentrate on what's going on. Instead of worrying about the future or regretting the past, you must be able to concentrate on the present moment. If you are always waiting for happiness, it will never come. You must be able to live in and enjoy the present moment so that you can really live your life instead of having it always control you.

Mindfulness is also about not being completely reactive to everything. Sometimes, it's necessary for you to just live in the moment instead of reacting to it. Instead of being overwhelmed by everything happening, you can learn to enjoy all of the details. Instead of letting your judgment rule you, you can go with the flow and just live. It can allow you to be more curious about the world around you instead of making immediate assumptions and letting your first thoughts influence your behavior. You will allow yourself to think more deeply and truly reflect on what is going on.

Mindfulness is a natural quality; it is instinctual to be mindful. One doesn't create mindfulness. It is, rather, a skill that must be sharpened and looked into. You must learn how to access your mindfulness and use it the best that you can. Much like building your biceps with arm exercises, you can strengthen your mindfulness with practice and certain techniques. You don't need to change yourself to develop mindfulness. You only need to bring out the best of yourself to use it well. Anyone can learn how to be more mindful. It is a way of living, and you can make it a part of your routine. It is easy to learn, and it has been proven to provide you with results. When you are mindful, you will be able to accept what is going on around you without adding your own judgment to it. It is a way of existing and appreciating what is happening.

Practicing Mindfulness

To build a habit, you must learn how to practice it. This is true for mindfulness. You must learn how to practice mindfulness so that you can begin practicing it in your life. Once you understand how to practice mindfulness, you can begin incorporating it into your life and make it a part of your routine. It can help you to improve your day and become more aware of your surroundings. With practice, mindfulness can come naturally to you. Although it will take effort at first, mindfulness can be a very simple habit to incorporate into your life.

To practice mindfulness, you will have to become more aware of your thoughts. Instead of allowing yourself to become absorbed in your worries, reacting to the world around you, or adding your judgment to each situation, you must become focused on the present and your life. It's important to develop a connection to the world around you and to be able to pay attention to how you feel and think. Mindfulness is about learning how to center your focus back to yourself instead of allowing yourself to get caught up in all of these thoughts.

You can practice mindfulness anywhere. You may choose to practice mindfulness during a routine activity, such as taking a shower or eating breakfast. Mindfulness is appropriate for any time, any place, and any person. You can choose to practice mindfulness while in motion or while staying still. What's important to remember is that you must be able to focus and shut off all distractions. When practicing mindfulness, you will instead focus on yourself and the world around you. It is as simple as paying attention to your senses. Focusing on your movement, breathing, anything that you smell, and more can make a huge difference. You are always going to smell, taste, hear, see, and feel. However, you aren't aware of your senses when you are lost in thought. It takes focus to be able to experience those senses. When you become mindful, you are more aware of what those senses are experiencing. You are tapping into what is already there but typically ignored.

Mindfulness also involves an awareness of your thoughts. You constantly have new thoughts, process them, judge them, and generate more thoughts from them. However, mindfulness involves observing your thoughts. Instead of processing them and judging them, you can listen to your thoughts. Just allow them to happen without feeling the need to do anything with them. Thoughts are constantly changing. Allow yourself to observe your thoughts moving from one subject to another without feeling the need to dive deeper and act on those thoughts. When you let your thoughts take over you, you will become overwhelmed, stressed, and anxious. By allowing yourself to be higher than those thoughts, you are separating yourself from your thoughts. You can be present in the moment instead of getting caught up in a path to the past or future. You will feel much better knowing that you have the power to control your thoughts, not let them control you.

Incorporating Mindfulness

Incorporating mindfulness into your life is easier than you would think. There are many ways that you can incorporate it into your life, as it is very versatile. Mindfulness can be practiced at home, at work, and even while you're out. It doesn't take any special tools or supplies to practice mindfulness, and it doesn't cost any money. While there are ways that you can add to your experience, such as getting a mindful meditation app or taking a class to become more mindful, you can practice mindfulness yourself whenever and wherever you would like. You may even pair it with activities that you already do every day.

One way that you may incorporate mindfulness into your life is by practicing it during every meal. Instead of mindlessly eating while going on your phone or watching the television, eat with mindfulness. Really take the time to focus on your food and eliminate other distractions. Not only will you feel more satisfied, but you will feel fuller and more nourished, which can eliminate the habit of overeating. You will never "miss" a meal, as you will be focused on your food. Take the time to enjoy every bite. Pay attention to how your food looks, tastes, and smells. This will help you to live in the present and enjoy your mealtime much more.

Start practicing mindfulness in every aspect of your routine. When you shower, enjoy the feeling of the water hitting your skin, really massage the shampoo into your scalp and relish in its refreshing, clean feeling. While driving, focus on the road; practice mindfulness instead of letting your mind wander. Choose activities that you can really put your focus on. Pick a hobby that you feel passionately about. It's great to have something that you can fully invest yourself into and distract yourself from your thoughts with. You may like reading and getting lost in a good book. Perhaps running is your way of focusing. No matter what it is, having a hobby that you really enjoy and can focus on is great. You may also want to try new things, as you can get lost in the thrill of newness. Travel somewhere new, try new foods, switch your routine around, or decorate your house. You will find that you are more mindful in the present when you experience new experiences.

You may also go for mindful walks. Get yourself outside in the fresh air and really enjoy it. Focus on your movement. Concentrate on how your feet connect with the ground and leave it again. Notice how your body supports you and your movement. Focus your attention on your surroundings. Listen to the bird's chirp. Watch the clouds move. Smell the fresh air. When you can develop an appreciation for the world around you, you will be more grateful for life and much happier.

Taking a moment every day to focus on your breathing is another great way to incorporate mindfulness into your life. Focus while taking deep breaths. This can assist you with relaxation and unwinding. It may also help you if you feel particularly stressed or overwhelmed by a certain situation that may have occurred. Become aware of the expansion that occurs when you breathe in and how your body contracts when you breathe out. Take deep breaths to really fill your body with new air, while exhaling to release all of the old air. Free yourself from your thoughts by focusing on your breathing.

Throughout your day, you may also choose to take pauses. Take a moment before you act to really let the action sink in. After sitting, take a pause to become aware of how your body feels in the chair. Before sleeping, pay attention to how your head feels on the pillow. Focus on the feeling of your blanket against your body. Enjoy the darkness and the peace it brings you. Pausing to enjoy the little moments in life will center you, clear your mind, and give you greater appreciation for the finer details that life offers you.

When others are talking to you, listen to them. Instead of getting lost in your thoughts or thinking about what you will say next, truly listen to what others are saying. Don't judge their words; let them sink in. Others will appreciate you more for it, and you will be able to absorb more information. Make it your goal to focus only on what others are saying when they are talking. Let their words resonate with you.

Meditation is a wonderful way to practice mindfulness. You may take some time to set aside for your daily meditation. Meditation can really help you to improve your mindfulness, and it is a great activity to add to your routine. You will feel a variety of benefits as a result of meditation.

Benefits of Mindfulness

Mindfulness can really help you. You will be able to focus on the present moment much more, instead of getting caught up in countless thoughts about the past or future. You will be able to make decisions better because of your increased ability to focus on what you would like to. You will feel more energized and motivated to accomplish all of your goals, as you will have a clearer mind and will stop focusing on the negatives in life. This will help you to accomplish more and be much more productive. Mindfulness will allow you to have access to greater opportunities and do more with your life.

You will also feel more energized. Instead of being weighed down by your thoughts and having little motivation to get out and accomplish your goals, you will feel a new sense of energy. You will be able to enjoy the present moment and have a greater appreciation for all that life offers you. This will also give you a new sense of hope and wonder. The world will seem like a more positive place that has so many wonderful details for you to become happy from. Mindfulness can really help you to live your fullest life.

Learning mindfulness is crucial. You need mindfulness to be able to take control of your thoughts instead of having them control you. This will allow you to minimize the overthinking, stress, and anxiety in your life. You will instead be able to be present in the moment. It will be much easier for you to observe your thoughts instead of getting caught up in them. Mindfulness is not a talent or a skill. It is, rather, something that we all possess but must tap into. Your senses will always work; your thoughts and feelings will always be present. However, you must be able to practice mindfulness and make a conscious effort to do so. It may not seem natural at first, yet it can really help you to improve your way of thinking.

You must understand what mindfulness is before you can begin to practice it. Mindfulness is focusing on the present and your thoughts, feelings, and surroundings instead of the countless distractions around you. To practice mindfulness, you must allow your body to focus and shift your concentration to the present. It is quite simple to incorporate mindfulness into your everyday life, as it is something you can practice at any time and in any place. It is free, easy, and can last as long as you would like. Mindfulness can truly benefit you, and it is worth it to try.

Chapter 6: Mastering Your Mind

You may struggle with your thoughts. Often, we let our thoughts control us, choose our actions, and bring us down. However, you must be able to control your thoughts. Mastering your mind will help you to become the leader of your emotions instead of feeling the need to react to and follow them. You will be able to focus more clearly on what matters to you instead of being swayed by your current thoughts. When you become a master of your mind, you will be able to face any situation that comes with you, and you will be much stronger overall. Becoming a master of your mind is something that you can practice and get better at, and it is a great way for you to improve your mental health and become more emotionally stable. You will feel less stressed as a result and overthink less.

To master your mind, you must learn how to control your thoughts. You must be able to take control of your thinking instead of letting it take control of you. You must also learn how to ride your emotional waves. Instead of letting your emotions control your actions, you must allow your emotions to happen naturally. Manipulating your mindset can also help you, as it will allow you to control the way you think. It's critical for you to not allow outside influences to destroy your thoughts. You are the one and only master of your mind. Don't let others bring you down.

Controlling Your Thinking

You are constantly thinking. Your brain is always shifting to a new subject; there's always something new to be thinking about. Often, our minds wander to places that we wish they wouldn't. It would make it so much easier if you were just able to control how you thought, right? Well, it's possible. Instead of dwelling on our worries, overthinking every situation, and wasting our time on thoughts that we wish we wouldn't, we may practice taking control over our thoughts. With time and practice, you can easily shift your thinking to more pleasant and productive thoughts. You may find yourself becoming stressed out as a result of your thoughts. However, you can help shift that so that you think better. You may shift your thinking to more important and meaningful thoughts as well. Instead of letting your mind wander, you can control where your mind goes. You may think what you want to so that you have the desired reaction to your thoughts.

To control your thoughts, you must be able to stop unwanted thoughts. Perhaps you are thinking something that stresses you out, makes you sad or causes frustration. To do so, you must catch yourself when you are thinking one of these thoughts and realize what the thought is and what effect it is having on you. When you feel yourself becoming upset, take a moment to reflect on yourself. What are you feeling at the moment? Are you stressed, mad, frustrated, sad, disappointed, anxious, or something else? Every feeling that you experience is caused by a thought that you have. Take a step back and identify what is causing that specific feeling. You may have to write down every single thought that you have or really scan your brain to determine what you're thinking.

After this, identify the further causes and effects. Why does that make you feel that way? Is it because of a negative event that happened similar to that? Did somebody else give you a bad feeling about an upcoming event? Determine why exactly you feel that way about whatever it is. There is almost always more than just the surface-level emotion and reasoning that is affecting you.

Once you have identified what caused this emotion, let it out. You may rant inside your head. You may choose to write it all down. You may even talk to somebody that you trust. Regardless, you should let out the emotion somehow; it is healthier to do so than to suppress your emotions. If you haven't dealt with a previous problem, you will need to now. Perhaps you are nervous about an upcoming interview because the last one you went to didn't work out well. Your brain will return to that disappointment until you have dealt with it and moved on. You must be able to separate the new situation from the old one. Those negative thoughts should not interfere with that. By dealing with the negative thoughts associated with that, you will remove yourself from that and be able to move on from the pain. You will also be able to get this mental image out of your mind.

It's also important to analyze what lies you are telling yourself and what the truth is. Because of that one negative event, you may tell yourself that you are incapable, bad at whatever it is, a failure, or that you won't succeed. These are all lies. Just because you didn't succeed once, that doesn't mean that you will never succeed. There are always obstacles that you must overcome and new opportunities that will arise. You may think of all of the successes that you have had. Although your mind will be drawn to the negative thoughts and failures, it is critical to also pay attention to all of the successes that you have had. This will show you that you are capable of.

Riding Your Emotional Waves

Emotions are just like waves. They come and go, and they're always changing. They go in different directions, have different intensities, and can be very powerful. Waves can be dangerous. If you go against the wave, you can be pushed against, pulled down, and even drown. This is similar to your emotions. If you try to suppress them or fight against them, you will not win. The emotions will take over and leave you feeling overwhelmed and defeated. However, it's possible for you to learn how to "surf" your emotions and use them to your advantage. Riding your waves instead of fighting against them can prove highly beneficial to you.

You must be able to anticipate the waves. Recognize that they will always come, and there is nothing that you can do to stop them. However, you may deal with them differently. A wave doesn't seem as overwhelming if you learn how to ride it. It only seems massive when you are about to be overcome by it. Understand that emotions will come and go and develop an appreciation for your emotions. This is what makes you yourself. There will be different emotions at different times and with different intensities.

You must be able to observe the wave before it comes. Acknowledge its existence and what type of wave it is.

There will be different waves, and you must be able to identify them and differentiate them. Recognize what type of emotion you are feeling. Do this without adding in your judgment. You must recognize that it is a part of who you are, but it doesn't define who you are. Every wave will be different, and you must be able to realize that. Determine how intense the wave is, as that will determine how you may best ride it.

You must be willing to ride the wave. Instead of letting it drown you, simply experience it. Realize that the wave will come and go. Just let it happen. Experience the emotion. Don't let it overpower you. If you fight against the emotion, you will only feel like you are drowning. Instead, let the wave happen. Realize that it won't last forever and riding it out will really help you. You may let yourself go through the stages of the wave so that you can experience it. You may just take some time to let it happen and do whatever feels natural.

Remember that there are always new waves coming. The wave that you are currently experiencing will not last forever. It will be replaced by a new wave. You will not be stuck on the same wave for the rest of your life. It will, in fact, make it easier for you to move onto the next wave if you learn to ride the current wave out. You may start to develop an excitement for the waves that you experience. It can be like a game for you. There is always a new wave coming; what will the next one be? Develop an excitement and appreciation for the variety of emotions that you experience. Don't view your emotions as either positive or negative. They are all part of the experience of life. You will have an emotion that you are riding right now, but that doesn't mean that you will be riding the same one next week, tomorrow, or even an hour from now. Be open to all of the emotions that you experience, as they will all be temporary. Experiencing one emotion may give you an even greater appreciation for another. Accept the wide variety of emotional waves that you ride.

Manipulating Your Mindset

Your mindset makes a huge difference in your way of thinking, your amount of motivation, your productivity, and your emotions. When you are able to shift your mindset to the one that you desire, you will be able to accomplish more and feel better. It is necessary for you to reframe your mindset so that you can accomplish your goals. Instead of reacting to everything, you must shift your way to respond to life. Obstacles are not what define you; it is how you overcome those obstacles that make you who you are and define how successful you will be.

One way to shift your mindset is to alter the way you view yourself. Instead of letting your mistakes define you, focus on your success and your potential for greater success. You must be able to be positive with yourself. Recognize that there is always room for improvement, and mistakes will always occur. New opportunities will always arise, and not every opportunity is meant for you. Realize that some missed opportunities will allow you the chance to experience others that you wouldn't have been able to otherwise. In general, you must shift your mindset regarding yourself. Remind yourself that you are capable of anything that you set your mind to, and you will be able to accomplish your goals.

You must also shift your mindset pertaining to outside situations. You may be unhappy with your current life at the moment, but you must be able to appreciate all of life: the good and bad. Shift your mindset to a growth mindset. There is always room for improvement, and you can make changes to your life to improve it. Never sell yourself short, as you always have the potential to make your life closer to the ideal image that you have for yourself.

Control Your Own Thoughts

We often let others control our thoughts. We can allow others to change our way of viewing the world and have them alter our emotions. You may be in a good mood, and one person may completely change your day (for better or for worse). It's important to not allow this to happen. You must be able to take full responsibility for your thoughts and emotions, and you shouldn't let others change that. Stay in control of your own thoughts. Although it's important to allow yourself to learn and grow from others, you must be able to still remain the ultimate master of your thoughts.

Regularly check in with yourself. Determine if how you are feeling is the result of someone else. If so, take a moment to separate yourself from the situation and reflect. Remember that everyone is entitled to their own thoughts. If someone tries to bring you down, respect that they may not be having the best day and handle your own emotions yourself. Stand up for yourself and your emotions. Avoid those who tend to focus on negative thoughts, drama, or the like. Stand up for your own beliefs and don't let others change those or bring you down.

Chapter 7: Stop Overthinking

One moment you're calm and everything is alright. Then, a thought hits your head. Perhaps it's a decision you're trying to make. Should you splurge on that piece of technology that you really want? Well, it'll be an investment so it's worth the money. But you could spend that money on other things. What else would you buy with that? What will others think of your purchase? Will you really use it? What if it breaks? But you could get the insurance. But then that's even more money. This could go on forever. You may find yourself overthinking every decision you have to make. It may seem nearly impossible for you to enjoy anything because you're too busy thinking about it instead of having a good time. You need to be able to live your life without letting your thoughts take over it. Overthinking can really become a burden to you.

You must know what overthinking means so that you know what it is. Everybody that experiences and struggles with overthinking will have a slight variation in the way that they experience it, but it's important to identify what it is. That way, you can become better at identifying if it is something that you struggle with. After that, you may learn how you can stop yourself from overthinking. You may also establish proper habits for preventing yourself from overthinking in the future. You may integrate these habits into your life so that you may think the way that you would like to.

What is Overthinking?

When you overthink, you are thinking instead of acting. You will spend too much time thinking and not enough time actually acting on those thoughts. Instead of being productive, you will spend your time repeating your thoughts. You will cycle through the same thoughts repeatedly, choosing to analyze and overanalyze the same thoughts over and over.

Overthinking will delay your action. It may be used as a form of procrastination, and it will serve as a way to prolong the planning process instead of acting on those thoughts and plans. It will consume your energy before you even have time to act. You will have trouble making decisions; it will either take much longer than necessary, or you won't be able to reach a decision at all. It can also be frustrating, as you will be unable to move on from a particular thought.

Overthinking can impair your relationships with others. You may struggle to understand what others are asking for, as you think beyond what they say. This can make communication harder, as you won't be as able to express your own thoughts. Understanding others can be a challenge as well because you may be too focused on a single detail instead of seeing the bigger picture. This can make it more difficult for you to plan your own future, as you may become stuck on one detail. It's important to be able to consider all factors in your life instead of becoming overly fixated on one or two details. This sort of thinking can become obsessive, as you may only focus on one detail and find yourself unable to move on from that.

Overthinking can cause you great stress and anxiety. You will be inefficient because you won't be able to accomplish what you want due to the fact that you are too focused on a particular thought. This thought can be an issue that you currently struggle with, a future problem to solve, or a past occurrence. Instead of actually solving your problem and fixing any issues, you will be too focused on thinking about those issues.

Often, one who overthinks will assume the worst. They will try to understand the inner workings of everything and come up with all of the potential outcomes for every situation. It is highly beneficial for you to be able to understand what overthinking entails so that you may understand if you struggle with overthinking.

Do You Struggle with Overthinking?

You must identify if you struggle with overthinking. Sometimes, you won't even realize that you struggle with it. There are a few signs that you may struggle with overthinking, and there are some typical characteristics of those that overthink that you may also experience in your life.

If you feel yourself constantly getting caught up in one thought, you may overthink. Those that overthink tend to get obsessed with the idea of a specific event, person, problem, or situation. They will constantly relive the moment, dwell on the problem, or find it hard to get over a certain emotion about someone or something. You may find yourself thinking of issues and being unable to concentrate on anything else, yet it can be hard to come up with a solution. You may try to distract yourself with another thought, activity, or action, but you can't help thinking about whatever it is; it always comes back to you.

You may also feel as if you are constantly worried or anxious. You find it hard to enjoy any events or activities because you are too focused on what can go wrong. There may always be questions in your head. What is going on? Why is that happening? What will happen next? Instead of being able to enjoy the moment and live in the present, you are completely fixated on one thought. It can be hard to really be present, and you may think that you are in a completely different world from those around you.

You may also find yourself dwelling on the negatives constantly. You think of your past mistakes and analyze what went wrong, why it went that way, and what you could have done to be better. It may be hard to imagine anything but good thoughts about yourself because you constantly think of what you could have or should have done in the past. Your thoughts may not be just of the past. You may overthink current problems and issues and the effects that they will have. You can imagine all of the possible outcomes and ways to handle those, yet you rarely reach a conclusion. Even if you do reach a conclusion, you will still be unsatisfied because you feel that there may be a better solution than you are aware of. Your thoughts may even lead to the future. What other issues will arise? How will you handle them? What will happen in the future? You feel like you can never escape the constant questions in your mind. You may also worry about things that you have no control over.

Throughout your day, you may find yourself over-analyzing everything. You may consider all of your interactions with people and relive conversations throughout the day. You may consider what you could have said or should have said. Perhaps you wish you hadn't said something because you think that the person may think differently of you or overthink themselves and be unimpressed with your unnecessary comment or response. You may try to analyze people's words beyond what they mean and try to piece together information to find a hidden or deeper meaning. This can lead to a distrust of people and a perceived dislike of people towards you. You may over-analyze every experience you have and consider the outcome, potential for improvement, and any issues that may arise as a result.

Additionally, you may find yourself exaggerating the meaning of people's words and actions and find that everything seems important to you. You may read signs that aren't there, yet you place importance on great details. It can be hard for you to relax, as you feel that there is constantly more to do and something to think about. As a result, it may prove difficult for you to focus on a task because your mind is elsewhere. It can be difficult to fall asleep because your mind is constantly on and thinking about something.

How to Stop Overthinking

Once you recognize that you struggle with overthinking, it's important to take action to stop yourself from doing so. You can really help yourself to improve your productivity, increase your concentration levels, and forming connections with others. There are a few different methods for how you can go about stopping yourself from overthinking and ending the constant cycle that you experience. Although it's common to overthink certain situations occasionally, those who struggle with more severe forms of overthinking and find themselves consistently doing so must take action so that they may take back control of their mind and life as a whole.

To start making changes, you must recognize that overthinking tendencies aren't permanent. It's possible to switch your way of thinking, and you can switch your tendencies to alter your mindset properly. You may use different strategies to overcome your habit of overthinking. By familiarizing yourself with several strategies, you may have a few methods to try for yourself.

One method to try is replacing the thought. You may choose a certain thought to go back to when you find yourself overthinking. You may also choose a certain theme for your thoughts. Instead of trying to change your way of thinking, you may simply think something else to get your mind off of it. This can help to improve your mood and get you out of the cycle that you feel stuck in.

However, this will require you to become more aware of your overthinking. You must be able to catch yourself when it happens so that you may make the necessary changes to change your habits. You may recognize the signs that you typically experience when you start overthinking. Some may have a specific thought or type of thought that they find themselves going back to again and again. You may find yourself having negative self-talk or thinking negatively. You may find yourself over-analyzing conversations, actions, or events that occur.

Whatever the go-to thought is, you may identify what it is so that you may catch yourself when it occurs. You may also have an emotion associated with your overthinking. Perhaps you feel especially stressed when you start overthinking. By learning how you react to your overthinking, you can stop yourself from doing so and be able to make changes to improve your life and eliminate your bad habits.

You may also try to alter your way of viewing situations. Instead of placing such an importance on every conversation you have, every place that you visit, and every event that you attend, you may be able to view it simply as another step in life. There is always room for improvement, and change is inevitable. Generate other interpretations of situations and events that occur. Find positivity instead of focusing on the negative aspects of everything. By reconstructing your way of thinking, you may easily help yourself to stop overthinking and live a much better life.

Habits for Preventing Overthinking

To really stop yourself from overthinking, you can integrate several habits into your life. This will help you to get over your tendency to overthink, and you will have an improved mindset. To really make a change in your life, you must be willing to change your mindset and develop a sense of self-awareness. You must be able to take a step back and realize when you are overthinking. Don't allow yourself to justify your overthinking or judge yourself for it. Instead, be willing to make some changes to yourself to improve your mindset and change your life for the better.

You may develop a distraction to prevent yourself from overthinking in the first place. You may tend to overthink because you have too much free time or lack engagement in the right activity. Become physically active can help your physical health, increase your energy levels, and help you to become fixated on one thing (that isn't overthinking). You may work on learning a new skill, such as cooking, learning a language, or learning how to play an instrument. You may develop a liking for a hobby that you feel passionately about. This can be anything from reading to drawing to horseback riding. Regardless, it's important to spend time doing something that you enjoy and are passionate about. You may even choose to volunteer; that way, you're finding something to do while helping others in the process.

Take some time to calm down. Recognize when you are overthinking and take some time to do what relaxes you the most. For some, this is taking a deep breath or stretching. For others, this may be a warm bath or shower. You may choose to read, meditate, get outside, or listen to music. Whatever you choose, remember that it is important to relax.

Take time each day to think about the bigger picture. Set goals for yourself and remind yourself what matters. Dwelling on the past won't help you in ten years. What will help is focusing on your goals and working towards achieving them. If you take the time to review your goals and ensure that you are making progress towards them, you will be more motivated to work towards achieving your goals. This will really help you to focus on what you need to when you find yourself overthinking. If you are passionate about your goals, you will place greater importance on them.

You must also acknowledge who you are. Remind yourself of your successes. Surround yourself with individuals who motivate and inspire you instead of bringing you down or inspiring negative thoughts. Clear negative thoughts out of your head and remind yourself that success is possible. You may achieve anything that you set your mind on. Celebrate your successes and remember to recognize all of the accomplishments that you have. Remember that mistakes are great opportunities for improving yourself. Every mistake that you make will help you to learn and grow. You may only improve yourself with greater time and knowledge.

It can be tough to struggle with overthinking. You may not be able to concentrate as well as you wish you should, and you may find yourself thinking about problems that you have no control over. It can be very stressful, as you will always feel worried and dwell on your mistakes and regrets in life. Talking to others can prove difficult, as you may feel that you are on a different level than they are. This can make connecting with others very difficult as well. Overthinking can result in great stress and anxiety.

You must be able to understand what overthinking is and what it entails. It's also important to understand what somebody who overthinks is like so that you may identify if you struggle with overthinking yourself. If you do struggle with overthinking, you must learn how to stop that habit so that you may live a life with fewer worries, stress, and anxiety. You can really help yourself to focus on what matters instead of overthinking and getting caught up in what doesn't. To really help yourself, you may integrate a few key habits to get you to prevent yourself from overthinking in the future and to have lasting results.

Chapter 8: Don't Let Others Bring You Down

We often give others way too much control of our own thoughts and actions. It can be easy to let somebody else ruin your day, change your opinion, or control your emotions. Yet, you must be able to overcome that. You are the ultimate master of your own mind. It is up to you how you want to feel. When you can learn how to shut others' opinions off and control your own thoughts, you will be much stronger. You are justified to think however you would like to, feel however you would like to, and act however you would like to. You shouldn't let others get in the way of your own happiness or success. Even so, we often let what others say get to us and can take things to heart. We spend our lives sacrificing our own happiness to please those around us. It's important to learn how to not let others bring you down.

You must learn how to defend yourself so that you don't let others take advantage of you. You must also stop others from taking over your mind. Don't let what others say get to you and be the sole master of your mind. It's critical that you surround yourself with the right people. The closest people in your life should support you, motivate you, and encourage you. You must be able to recognize unnecessary negativity from others and separate yourself from it. This is important so that you can live your best life.

How to Defend Yourself

When we let others control how we feel and bring us down, we can really let words get to our heads. You must be able to defend yourself against others' words. People aren't always kind. They don't always think about their words before they say them out loud. It's important to be able to defend yourself from others, as people will try to take advantage of you and test their limits for what they can say to you. Some get enjoyment out of criticizing others or do it as a result of being insecure themselves. You must be able to verbally defend yourself so that you don't let others harm you with their words.

You must be able to separate yourself from the words of others. People say rotten things because they are having a bad day and taking their emotions out on you. They may not realize that what they say will affect you badly. It's important to not allow others to ruin your self-image or affect the way you think. It's easier said than done to not take things personally, however.

There are many reasons why you shouldn't take what others say personally. However, you must be able to take a step back and realize this. When you experience verbal insults or abuse, it can be extremely difficult to not get hurt by it. It can feel very individual and hurt more than physical pain. We may feel obligated to hide our hurt, as the pain doesn't leave a physical mark. However, you must be able to recognize that you can defend yourself from the insults of others. You must be able to recognize when it is time to take action, as those who insult others often don't realize they are or consider the effect that they have on others. You must learn how to properly defend yourself when this happens.

The first step is recognizing when someone is attacking you verbally. This person may be unintentionally saying things that hurt you, or they may target you. Those that attack others with their words want to belittle you and make you feel controlled by them. They want you to feel hurt and weak. You must recognize that these attacks shouldn't be ignored; you must defend yourself.

To defend yourself, you must remain calm and confident. If the individual believes that you are vulnerable, they will not respect you. If they feel that you are attacking them, they will only increase their level of attack. Analyze what their intent is and act appropriately. If they are hurting you, tell them. It is okay to let someone know that their remarks are inappropriate or hurtful. You may even tell them that you do not wish to continue the conversation. Let them know how you feel. If they respect you and your feelings, they will stop. This may help them to realize that what they are saying is inappropriate. For those that don't stop, remove yourself from the situation. It is okay to do this, as you must respect yourself and get away from others who don't give you the same respect.

After this, forgive the person. Realize that they made a mistake, and it is okay. They do not have the right to make you feel bad, and there is always a reason for their attacks. Perhaps they had a bad childhood and grew up with poor values that they never abandoned. They may just struggle with coping with their emotions and have chosen to take them out on you. Forgive others, and you will feel better about yourself.

Take Control of Your Mind

It's common to let others control everything you do. You may let others' opinions influence yours. You may lose motivation as a result of unmotivated people around you. It's important to take control of your own mind and not let others change the person who you are; you must stay true to yourself.

Often, we absorb the energy of those around us and become who we surround ourselves with. You may feel tempted to absorb the negative energy of those around you, and this can make it difficult for you to think positively yourself. You may be having a wonderful day until a certain person puts their problems on you. This won't help you at all. When this happens, you must remove yourself from the situation so that you can be the best person that you can. Don't let others bring you down; avoid those who consistently do so. Similarly, you must be able to remove yourself from those who speak negatively about others. Gossip and drama will do nothing but hurt others. If you avoid getting involved with gossip and drama, you will have better relationships with others, gain the trust of others, and be more respected.

You must also not let others change your beliefs. Religious and political beliefs are typically the most personal beliefs that one holds, and everyone deserves the right to have their beliefs respected. It is okay to have different beliefs from others; that's what makes each individual special. When others fail to respect your beliefs, however, it is not helpful for you. You must not let others question your beliefs. This doesn't mean that you should shut off the beliefs of others. You likely have beliefs that are constantly changing as you learn more and hearing the beliefs of others can inspire you and help you to grow as a person. Yet, you must not allow anybody to force their beliefs on you or try to change your beliefs just because they disagree with you. Respectfully defend yourself or withdraw yourself from the situation if anyone tries to do so yet remain open-minded when listening to others.

Similarly, you should not let others force their judgment of you upon you. Often, others will criticize your goals. They may tell you what they think your limits are, and this can be really disappointing. Remember what your values are and take time regularly to remind yourself of them. Check with your goals and your progress towards them. If you have a passion for something, don't let anyone tell you that it isn't special or interesting. All that matters is what you think. You will be happiest when you fulfill your own desires, dreams, and goals. It's important to stay true to your personality. If you are happy with yourself, then you will be happiest in life. Pleasing others should not be your top priority. Although you may always ask for the opinions of others, you shouldn't change yourself based on every little thing that somebody says.

Don't let others take advantage of you. There are many that try to dump their problems on you and get solutions from you without doing anything in return. This will only leave you feeling used and worthless. Take control of your mind and your life. Don't allow yourself to be used. You shouldn't give people that power. Sometimes, it can feel good to help others. It will give you satisfaction knowing that you are making someone else happy. You will find yourself only living your life for others if you do so. You will end up living your life for others instead of for yourself. Remember, though, that everyone has their own life. You are the only one that's living your specific life, so you must respect yourself. Don't let others take power away from you and stop you from making your own decisions or doing what makes you happy.

Choosing the Right People

Surrounding yourself with the right people can really change your life. Most of your motivation, personality, and decision-making is influenced by the few people that you interact the most with. You will likely seek their support and ask for their advice. Subconsciously, you will also adopt a lot of those individuals' mannerisms. Surround yourself with the people that you want to be more like. Pick friends that you admire. Pick a partner that motivates you to be your best self. Try to work with people that help you to accomplish the most. The people you choose in life can make you a better person.

Each person is in your life for a specific reason. You don't have to expect anybody to be perfect or to have the exact goals and dreams that you have. Appreciate everyone in your life and the purpose that they serve in your life. Although it is ideal to have someone with similar values and goals as you so that you can motivate each other, you can also have friends to enjoy your hobbies with. You may have people that you work well with, people that you can talk to, and people that you spend time with. Don't spend your time over-analyzing everybody and searching for the perfect friend, co-worker, or partner. Nobody is perfect. If you are surrounding yourself with people who make you feel good and make you a better person, you are doing well. Everyone is special, and everyone has a different purpose. Always keep an open mind with people.

When picking who you develop a relationship with, look for those who you can really establish a connection with. This can be a similar interest or belief. You may both get along really well and be comfortable around each other. It's important to have people in your life that you can be completely yourself around and feel comfortable with. For those who you wish to establish a long-term connection with, you must feel an emotional bond. Although surface-level acquaintances are fine to have, they typically don't involve anything more than small talk. Having someone that you trust can make for a better and longer relationship, and you will feel more emotionally nourished as a result. The individual should listen to you, understand you, and feel comfortable with you. You should feel comfortable around them and willing to share your thoughts with them.

Although it can be nice to surround yourself with people that are similar to you, it's also important to have those that are different from you in your life. You should build relationships with people that are strong in areas that you are weak. Build relationships with people that you admire or want to be more like. These people can help you grow, give you advice, and make you better. You will be a much better-rounded person as a result. You may even be able to help each other. That can form a better bond between you as a result.

Removing the Wrong People

You must be able to recognize unnecessary negativity from others and separate yourself from it, as this will help you to grow as a person and be much happier. There are people in the world that will do nothing but bring you down. You may feel bad for them and choose to keep them in your life out of sympathy, yet you must be able to put yourself first and do what benefits you and will make your life better. Some people can be very toxic and hold you back from being the best version of yourself possible. It's okay and actually very beneficial for you to remove toxic and negative people from your life.

For those that you are close with, you may be able to confront them. Perhaps you can let them know (in a respectful way) that they may need to work on their negativity. They may not even realize the way that they act, and it will take someone like yourself to let them know how they appear to others. This is a way to attempt to keep someone in your life that is negative. Instead of suddenly cutting them off, you are giving them a chance to improve and redeem themselves. Their response to you will also reveal a lot about their character. If they are unable to receive constructive criticism or don't like what you said, this may not be the best person to have in your life. You should be surrounding yourself with people who you can be open to and trust.

You may have people that you deal with in real life that are negative, yet there are also many who take their negativity online. If you follow, are friends with, or otherwise interact with those that are negative on social media, it can be very draining. People may post about their negative views on life and constantly complain about their problems, and this can be irritating to read about. It may also negatively affect you. For those in your life that take their complaining, negativity, and toxic ways online, you should learn to avoid them. It's okay to unfollow, unfriend, or unsubscribe from those that don't motivate you to be the best person you can be. Those that you follow online should inspire you and make you happy. If you find yourself become frustrated, annoyed, or otherwise unhappy because of somebody online, remove them from your feed or unfollow them.

For those that bring you down in real life, you should remove them from your life. You are not obligated to say yes to plans. You don't have to go out of your way to talk to anybody. Don't feel pressured to become friends with somebody just because you feel like you should. You can remain civil with people without being their best friend. Of course, building relationships with others is an essential part of your life; it's important for both your own happiness and for your business endeavors. However, don't put those that bring you down on a pedestal.

You must be able to take control of your mind and not let others do so for you. Learn how to defend yourself against others' words so that you can't let them bring you down. It's important to be able to stick up for yourself and stay true to what you believe despite what others say or think. You also need to surround yourself with the right people. Eliminating negative people in your life is a great way to eliminate negativity as a whole from your life. Surrounding yourself with people that you trust, admire, and feel comfortable with can really help you to succeed. Others can have a huge effect on you, so you must be able to take control of your life.

Chapter 9: Eliminate Stress

Stress can really wear you out. It causes you to panic, feel unmotivated, and be unhappy in general. It's important for you to be able to eliminate stress so that you can accomplish more, feel happier, and be more present in your life. Just the word "stress" can bring up emotions that you don't feel comfortable with. It is a common problem for most, and many struggle with dealing with their stress and preventing further stress in the future. You must learn how to fight against stress when it happens so that you can deal with it properly and feel better. There are also a few strategies to help you reduce stress in the future. This will prevent you from becoming stressed out in the first place. Practicing self-care and stress-relieving habits can really help you to live a more stress-free life and calm down after you start to feel stressed. You can also recognize what stresses you out so that you may eliminate that from your life and avoid becoming stressed out by that in the future.

How to Fight Against Stress

Stress can be, well, stressful! It can be very difficult to handle and have to deal with. Stress can take over your life and leave you feeling unmotivated. You won't be able to focus or put your all into anything because you will be too focused on the stress. When you feel stressed, it can be hard to think clearly and act properly to fight against your stress. You may try to suppress your stress and continue with the activity you are currently engaged in. However, you must be able to know how to properly fight against your stress once it's there.

A little stress here and there is sometimes necessary. It may be helpful to experience a bit of urgency so that you feel like the task at hand is more important and requires your immediate attention. When you feel completely overwhelmed by your stress, though, you need to act upon that and listen to the signals that your body is sending you. When you are doing something that is causing you great stress, step away from the activity. Withdraw yourself peacefully and just take a moment to breathe. You may worry that this will only worsen it, as you will feel like you are being unproductive or wasting your time. However, it's necessary for you to take a step back. Taking a small break can really help you to take a breath and stop yourself from becoming too overwhelmed. After your break, you will come back feeling much better than you did before, and you will accomplish much more. This is better than forcing yourself to continue while you are stressed, as you won't be able to accomplish anything since your mind won't be in the right place.

Taking a small break may not be the right way for you to cope with your stress. Everyone deals with their feelings and emotions differently, and you must try several ways to cope with your stress to see which way works best for you. When you feel stressed, the best solution may be for you to talk to somebody about what is bothering you. You may feel better after writing down everything that is stressing you out. Perhaps you prefer to distract yourself with another activity, such as a hobby or going for a walk outside. See what works best for you when you are stressed and stick to that. Everyone will deal with their stress differently. What's important to remember, however, is that you can't ignore your stress; that won't help it or make it go away.

Strategies to Reduce Stress

Although it's important to know what to do once you get to the point where you are overly stressed, it's just as important (if not, more important) to know how to prevent stress from occurring in the first place. There are some strategies that you may follow to reduce the stress that you have in your life.

One way to reduce your stress is by switching your mindset. By becoming more positive about the events in your life, you may view life in a better life. Instead of becoming stressed out about the potential of failure, you may accept that mistakes are great opportunities to learn and will make you a better and stronger person. You may also accept the fact that not everything is within your control. It is pointless to stress out about events, circumstances, or people that you have no control over. Often, frustration is not beneficial or productive.

You must also accept that your feelings are valid. Although they may not be logical or occur at a desired time, your emotions will always be valid. You must respect yourself and act appropriately when you are upset. If you choose to ignore how you are feeling, you will only make things worse for yourself. Suppressing your emotions may work for a short amount of time, but those feelings will most certainly resurface, and they will affect you even if you don't realize it. Stress can hold you back from your full potential.

You may also try relaxing. This will really help you to wind down and take a step back from whatever is stressing you out. When you take time to relax, you will feel much better and will be able to focus on yourself and making yourself feel happy. Cooling down will really help you to feel much better. When you're stressed, you may feel very anxious, fidgety, or all over the place. Relaxing can snap you back to reality and make you realize that it's important for you to calm down and take a breath. You'll feel better for it.

Take care of your physical health. When you eat properly, you will feel more energized, motivated, and happy. You will be able to concentrate better. When you sleep properly, your body will be refreshed and have enough energy to get you through the day. Exercising can make you feel better, and you will be in better shape. Your body will be able to handle more, and you will feel better about yourself. Avoid relying on alcohol or drugs, as those can increase your stress and damage your body, especially when they are overused. Your physical health can help you to feel better and think more clearly.

You must also care for your mental health. Learn how to say "no" to what stresses you out. If your schedule is already packed, you don't have to feel obligated to say "yes" to any plans. Respect yourself and your body. Socialize regularly and build lasting relationships with others. Having people around that love and care about you can help you to feel happier and less stressed. You can feel more supported and less lonely, too. Remember to listen to your body and what it is trying to tell you about your feelings.

Establishing Stress-Relieving Habits

Establishing proper habits can really help you to relieve your stress. Stress is a very common issue that many struggle with, and it can be quite simple to add a few healthy habits to your routine. A little bit of effort goes a long way. By adding a few tweaks to your routine, you can help to feel calmer and prevent yourself from stressing in the future. Your mental health as a whole will be better. You will be able to form better relationships with others, accomplish more throughout the day, and make better progress towards achieving your goals by establishing a few healthy habits.

One habit that you may practice is self-care. Self-care is going out of the way to take time for yourself. Many avoid practicing self-care because they view it as selfish. It most certainly is not selfish. Self-care can help you to feel much better and is necessary for taking care of yourself properly. When you practice self-care, you will be able to focus on yourself and what makes you happy. Do something that makes you feel better. For some, this might be relaxing and taking a warm bath or a long shower. It may be doing something you love, such as writing or another hobby of yours. No matter what, you must take time for yourself. Do this for a little each day, and you will feel better. It will give you a sense of purpose and taking time to make yourself happy can make you feel like you matter more. It's also just as important to spend time with others as it is to spend time on yourself. Being around those who you can smile and laugh with can really help you to be happier and get lost in the moment. This will distract you from your stress and help you to realize that life is full of positivity. Pick at least one way each day to practice self-care.

Sunday	Monday	Tuesday	Wednesday	Thursday	Friday	Saturday
Bike ride	Bath	Unplug and read	Dance class	Writing	Walk	Movie night

To relieve your stress, you may also satisfy your senses. The right smells can be very relaxing. You may light a candle or use essential oils to provide yourself with a relaxing smell. Having an environment that relaxes you can also help you to be less stressed. Take some time each day to clean up and ensure that everything is tidy. You may also switch around your space regularly to inspire yourself to be more creative.

You should also find a hobby to dedicate yourself to. Choose something that you are passionate about. It can help you to stay focused on what you love, and you will be able to do something that you enjoy as well. Regularly devote your time to your hobby. You may take classes or lessons, join a club, or put aside time each day or week to involve yourself in your hobby. Your hobby can also be something that you can rely on to get you focused when you are feeling stressed. It can be the one thing that makes you happy, and you can always go to when you need it.

Recognize What Stresses You Out

Learning to recognize what stresses you out can make a huge impact on your stress levels. When you are able to pinpoint what is causing you stress, you can make a move to eliminate that from your life and reduce the stress that it causes you. You must be able to learn more about yourself and listen to your brain. Often, we ignore the signs that our mind is giving us. When you learn how to tune in to those thoughts, you can become much more aware of your emotions and why you feel the way that you do. This will help you to lead the happiest life that you can, as you will be doing what makes you happy and avoiding what doesn't.

First, you must learn how and when to reflect. When you are feeling stressed, take some time to really step back and analyze what you feel and why. Consider every possible reason that you may feel stressed. It may help you to write everything down or talk to someone about it. Try to imagine every possible reason why you are feeling the way that you do. Then, think about what effect this has on you. What are you feeling, why are you feeling that way, and what is the effect of feeling that way? After you can answer these questions, you may move on. Figure out how to effectively solve the feelings that you have. Maybe you like to go for a run when you're angry. Find what helps you to cope with the emotions that you feel and do it.

You may consider a few aspects when trying to think about what is stressing you out. Consider if anybody is stressing you out. Is there something that somebody said that's bothering you? Has somebody released their negativity onto you? Perhaps you feel inferior to somebody else or are experiencing jealousy. Has your relationship with anybody been particularly strained lately? Consider if any person in your life is stressing you out. You may choose to confront them about it or distance yourself from them for the moment.

Consider if any event is causing you stress. Is there a deadline coming up that you feel stressed about? Is there an event happening soon that is stressing you out? Maybe you are stressed about a past event. Consider if this is the cause of your stress. Remind yourself that past mistakes help you to grow; dwelling on them won't change them. The future is out of your control. You can work hard now to make it the best you can, but you can't predict the future. Life is full of surprises.

Lastly, consider if you are stressing yourself out. Are you feeling unmotivated? Are you insecure? Perhaps your self-image is struggling, and you don't feel confident in yourself. Remind yourself of your successes and seek the help of others if needed. It's important to always love yourself and respect yourself. Consider if this is what's stressing you out.

Eliminating stress can really help you out. Because stress is a common distraction, it can help you accomplish much more throughout your day. When you live a stress-free life, you will be able to focus on what matters instead of only thinking about what is stressing you out. You will also be happier overall. Stress can cause a variety of negative emotions. You may feel frustrated that you can't properly deal with everything happening. It's also common to feel worthless, hopeless, and unmotivated. By eliminating stress, you're able to eliminate these emotions and focus on your happiness instead. Fighting against stress will help you to eliminate these emotions, and you may even form better relationships with those around you. You will be able to think more clearly and focus on happiness and positivity more as a result. There are a few strategies to reducing your stress and stopping yourself from becoming stressed in the first place. Practicing self-care and other habits that relieve your stress can really help you to feel more relaxed and to think more clearly. By recognizing what stresses you out, you can prevent yourself from becoming stressed and remove certain things from your life.

Chapter 10: Tips and Tricks

To maximize your progress, there are a few additional tips and tricks for you to be aware of. These will help you to make better progress towards your goals and to make it easier for you to accomplish what you want to. You may work on improving your health, as it affects everything you do. Having the proper mindset will also really help you, as you can accomplish more and feel better when you have the proper mindset. You may also learn some additional tips and tricks regarding goal-setting and how to establish new habits.

Improving Your Health

You may learn how to improve your mental and physical health. Your health affects everything that you do. When you are physically healthy, you will have more motivation and energy, so you can accomplish more. You will feel better and feel more motivated to get out and make progress towards achieving your goals. Your physical health directly affects your mental health. If you are physically healthy, you will feel more confident. Having good physical health will also help you to recognize that you are capable of achieving your goals. When you are mentally healthy, you will be less stressed and anxious. You won't worry as much, and you will be able to focus more on what's important. You will be in a better place and be able to make decisions better. You will also improve your relationships with others and communicate more effectively. The following are some tips and tricks for improving your health.

Find out if you are the proper weight. The best way to do so is to consult a medical professional. If you are overweight or obese, you are greatly increasing your risk for a variety of health problems, and you must take action and make progress towards being your ideal weight. Being overweight can increase your risk for health conditions, as well as physical injuries and pain. When you are not physically healthy, you will not feel as well and will feel unmotivated to get out and accomplish your goals. You may also feel self-conscious and lack confidence in yourself as a result.

Practice morning and nighttime routines. By having a set routine in the morning, you are starting off on the right foot and setting yourself up for success. It will get you in the right headspace to be productive throughout the day. You may take a shower, eat breakfast, go for a run, go over your to-do list, or whatever it is that helps you to get motivated and ready for the day. Having a nighttime routine is great so that you can unwind, relax, and get ready for bed. It will help you to fall asleep faster and stay asleep throughout the night. This can really help you if you are stressed, anxious, or tend to overthink. You may also establish a skincare routine so that you take care of your skin properly. Don't forget to use sunscreen every day as well so that you can protect your skin daily.

There are some other simple ways to improve your health. Going to bed at a decent time can help you to get a proper amount of sleep. Having good posture can improve your muscular health. Doing puzzles and reading books are great ways to stimulate your mind. Swapping out junk food for more nourishing food will fuel your body more effectively. Making simple exercise swaps such as taking the stairs instead of the elevator and parking farther will get you to exercise a bit more. Also, remember to stretch regularly (and after exercising) to avoid injury and increase your flexibility.

Having the Proper Mindset

Your mindset can make or break you. If you have the proper mindset, you will view life much more positively. You will be able to bounce back quickly after hitting an obstacle or having an issue. You will see the world as a much more positive place with infinite room to grow and improve. It will also be easier for you to find motivation and push yourself to work towards your goals. You will enjoy learning and bettering yourself, and it will be easy for you to establish new habits and live a healthier life. The proper mindset can make a world of difference for you.

To improve your mindset, you can start off your day with positive affirmations. Tell yourself how wonderful you are. Remind yourself of your achievements and the strengths that you have. You may also focus on what you are grateful for and everything good in your life. Remember to laugh. To cope with bad situations, find humor, and enjoy a good laugh. Life doesn't have to be so serious, after all. Remember that failures make the greatest lessons, and you can learn from your mistakes. Think highly of yourself and learn to live with no regrets. Even if you could have done something, you didn't. Everything happens for a reason, and everything that has happened in the past has led to this moment. Appreciate that and learn to focus on the present instead of the past (or worrying about the future). Surround yourself with people that have the mindset that you want.

To work on improving your mindset, you may practice breathing, which will allow you to focus more and simply relax. You may also reflect on your thoughts to check your emotions. Write down anything you are thinking: your worries, anything you need to do, what you love about life, your goals, and what you're grateful for. Sometimes, it's good to have your thoughts written down. Always remember to set goals for the next day so that you have something to work towards and achieve. Switch up what you listen to. Instead of listening to the news, listen to music so that you can focus on your thoughts instead of the thoughts of others. Maybe your drive to work is usually silent. In that case, you may want to try a podcast to inspire you. Listen to what makes you feel happy and motivated.

Focus on your language. Do you use words that you are proud of? Is there a way to change the way you speak to be more positive? Become mindful of this. Start reading! You can educate yourself and learn about a new topic or get sucked into a good story and lose yourself in the book. Learn what emotional outlet works for you. Instead of suppressing your emotions, practice dealing with them in a healthy way. Reward yourself for your successes. When you accomplish a goal, make good progress, or have another success, take time to recognize your achievement and reward yourself for your good work. This will keep you motivated and ready to accomplish more. You will start associating your goals with happiness and rewards. Remember to smile. Surround yourself with people that make you laugh and smile and remember to do what makes you happy.

Setting Goals and Establishing New Habits

Setting goals can be hard! You may not know where to start, what you want to accomplish, or how to set your goals properly. Establishing habits may also be tricky, as you must incorporate something new into your life and stick with it. The following are some tips and tricks for helping you with improving these.

To properly set goals, it's important to choose goals that you feel passionately about. If you don't care about a goal, you're not likely to stick with it. The typical proper goal is SMART. It should be specific, measurable, attainable, relevant, and time-bound. Be specific about what you want. Set a goal that you can measure your progress. Make sure it is realistic for you to attain. Make it relevant to your interests and passions. Give yourself time to achieve that goal. Doing these will help you to properly set a goal so that you may achieve it.

There are a few categories for goals that you may set for yourself. You may set educational goals so that you may learn more. This can pertain to college, classes, lessons, or professional certifications and licenses. You may also set health goals. This can include exercising, eating well, sleeping better, and taking care of your mental health. Relationship goals can help you to have better relationships in business, your romantic life, with family, and with friends. Personal development goals will help you to grow and improve yourself. This can be learning a new language, getting started with a new hobby, or otherwise improving yourself. You may set career goals to further yourself with your career. Financial goals may deal with saving, investing, or making more money. Spiritual goals can pertain to mindfulness, meditation, or religion. Psychological goals are important for remaining emotionally stable and improving your mindset. These are all types of goals that you can set for yourself.

For getting started with new habits, you will have to make a change and make that change a part of your life. It will require you to get used to it and make it a natural part of your daily routine. To properly form habits, you should focus on only one to three habits at once. Any more will overwhelm you, and you won't be able to fully dedicate yourself to them. Commit for at least thirty days. This is how long it will take for you to get used to your new habit or habits. Give yourself a reminder. Perhaps one activity that you already do should go along with your new habit. You may have to give yourself reminders for your new habit. Don't expect too much at once. You may ease into the new habit and gradually make progress towards it. Plan for failure, and know what you will do when you face obstacles and how you won't let them get in your way. Tell others about your habit so they may hold you accountable for it. Reward yourself for making progress towards your habit. Finally, remember that you can change yourself. Accept and welcome change into your life. You can't get better if you don't make a change.

Conclusion

Thank you for making it through to the end of *Stop Overthinking;* let's hope it was informative and able to provide you with all of the tools you need to achieve your goals of stopping your overthinking habits. Hopefully, you are also able to start the process of decluttering your mind as well. Additionally, let's hope you are able to relieve any anxiety you may have and learn how to manage your stress more effectively. This book will have also helped you to eliminate negativity in your life, control your thoughts, and stop complaining. By establishing new habits and learning some strategies for improving yourself, you may achieve new results and think the way that you want to. You will think more clearly, which will allow you to focus on achieving your goals and enjoying your life.

The next step is to integrate those habits into your life. Start by working on your focus. You may take some time to declutter, stop multi-tasking, and write down a schedule for yourself to stick to. Also, write down to-do lists for yourself to practice prioritizing and regularly do brain dumps to keep your thoughts written down. To stop worrying, you can write down all of your potential worries, take time to reflect, and talk to others. You may practice some habits to relieve your anxiety. Try taking care of your physical health, taking time to relax, and being more conscious of your mental health. Erasing negativity can be achieved by practicing good habits. You should remove negative people and places from your life, eliminate negativity from your routine, and stop yourself from complaining. You may also find more positivity in life and eliminate anything else that causes you negativity.

Practicing mindfulness can also be done to help you and your mental health. You may make a conscious effort to be more mindful, or you may choose an activity to help you with your mindfulness, such as yoga or meditation.

Work on mastering your mind. Identify what you are thinking and why you are thinking that. Remember to ride your emotional waves, think more positively, and maintain control of your thoughts. To stop overthinking, you can replace your thoughts, alter your way of viewing situations, and distract yourself. You may also take time to calm down, think about the bigger picture, and remind yourself of your positive aspects. Don't let others bring you down. Take time to practice defending yourself, staying true to your beliefs, and considering if you're surrounding yourself with the right people. You may work on eliminating stress in your life by relaxing, accepting your feelings, and practicing self-care. You may also find a hobby to stick to and satisfy your senses. Work on setting goals and establishing new habits for yourself, as well as working on improving your health and having the proper mindset. These will all help you to be better.

Finally, if you found this book useful in any way, a review on Amazon is always appreciated!

Powerful Motivational Quotes to Unlock Your Potential

"Don't let your thoughts control you, take control of your thoughts."

"Overthinking is the enemy of progress."

"Stop thinking and start doing."

"Action is the antidote to overthinking."

"Don't let your mind create problems that don't exist."

"Worrying won't change the outcome, so focus on what you can control"

"Don't let your thoughts paralyze you, take a step forward"

"The more you think, the harder it gets to act. So act now"

"You can't control everything, so stop trying to"

"Trust your instincts, they won't lead you astray"

"Overthinking is a waste of time and energy"

"Focus on the present moment, not the past or future"

"Sometimes the best decision is the one you make without thinking"

"Don't let your thoughts limit your potential"

"Your thoughts don't define you, your actions do"

"Trust yourself and your abilities, you've got this"

"Overthinking won't solve anything, take action instead"

"The more you think, the less you do"

"Don't let your thoughts hold you back from achieving your dreams"

"There's no such thing as failure, only learning opportunities"

"Don't let fear and doubt control you, believe in yourself"

"Stop waiting for the perfect moment, make the moment perfect"

"Take one step at a time, you'll get there eventually"

"Focus on the solution, not the problem"

"Success comes from taking action, not from overthinking"

"Don't let your mind convince you that you're not good enough"

"Overthinking is like quicksand, the more you struggle, the deeper you sink"

"Believe in yourself, you're capable of achieving great things"

"Don't let your thoughts dictate your life, take control"

"It's okay to make mistakes, they help you grow and learn"

"The best way to predict the future is to create it"

"Stop doubting yourself, you're stronger than you think"

"Focus on progress, not perfection"

"The only thing standing between you and success is yourself"

"Don't let your thoughts become your worst enemy"

"Believe in your abilities, you're capable of achieving anything you set your mind to"

"Don't let your thoughts create roadblocks, find a way around them"

"Overthinking is a habit, break it and start living"

"Take risks, they can lead to great rewards"

"Don't let your thoughts limit your potential"

"You can't change the past, so focus on the present and future"

"Don't let fear hold you back, embrace it and move forward"

"Don't let your thoughts paralyze you, take a step forward"

"You're stronger than you think, don't let overthinking bring you down"

"Don't wait for someone else to make your dreams come true, make them happen yourself"

"Stop worrying about what others think, focus on your own goals and dreams"

"Believe in yourself, you have the power to make things happen"

"Take action, even if it's a small step"

"Don't let your thoughts create obstacles, find a way to overcome them"

FREE e-book

"Congratulations on completing 'Stop Overthinking'! We hope that this guide has provided you with valuable insights and practical tips for decluttering your mind, mastering your emotions, and unlocking your full potential.

As a token of our appreciation, we would like to offer you a FREE e-book from the same author, Zachary Miller. Simply scan the QR code on this page to access your free copy.

Thank you for choosing 'Stop Overthinking' as your guide towards a more mindful and positive life. We wish you all the best on your journey towards personal growth and success!"

Made in the USA
Monee, IL
31 July 2023